MW01469268

This book belongs too:

____

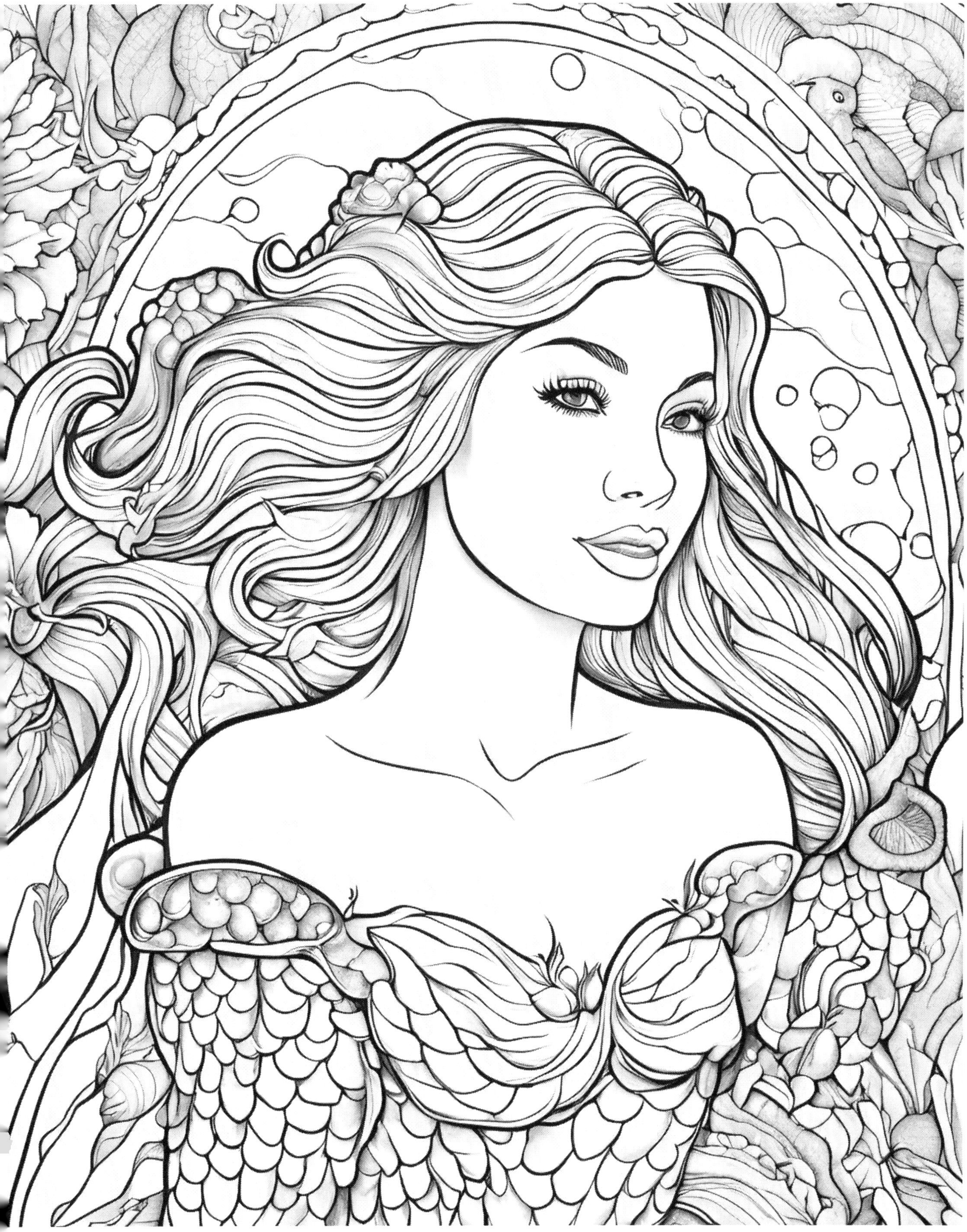

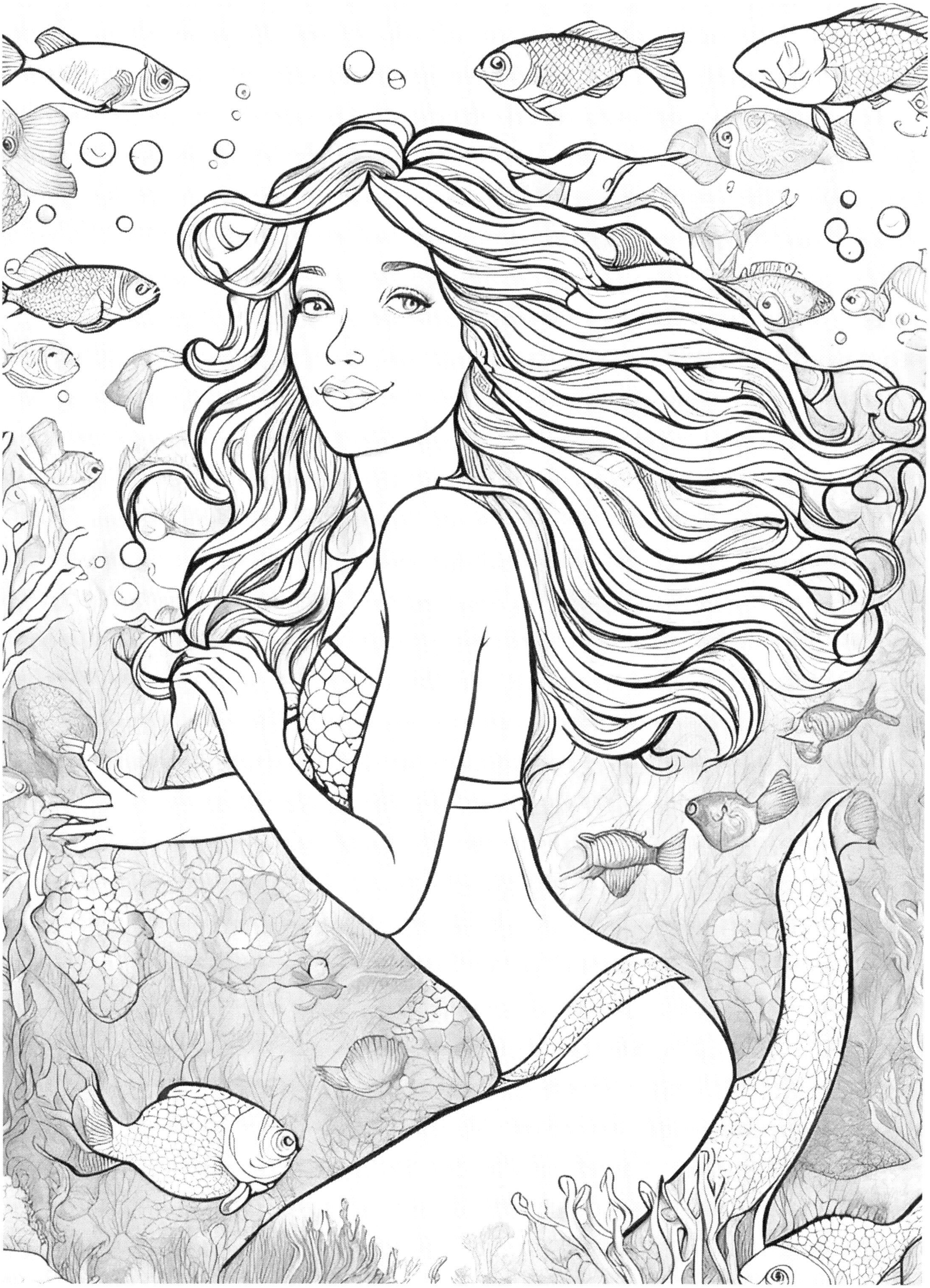

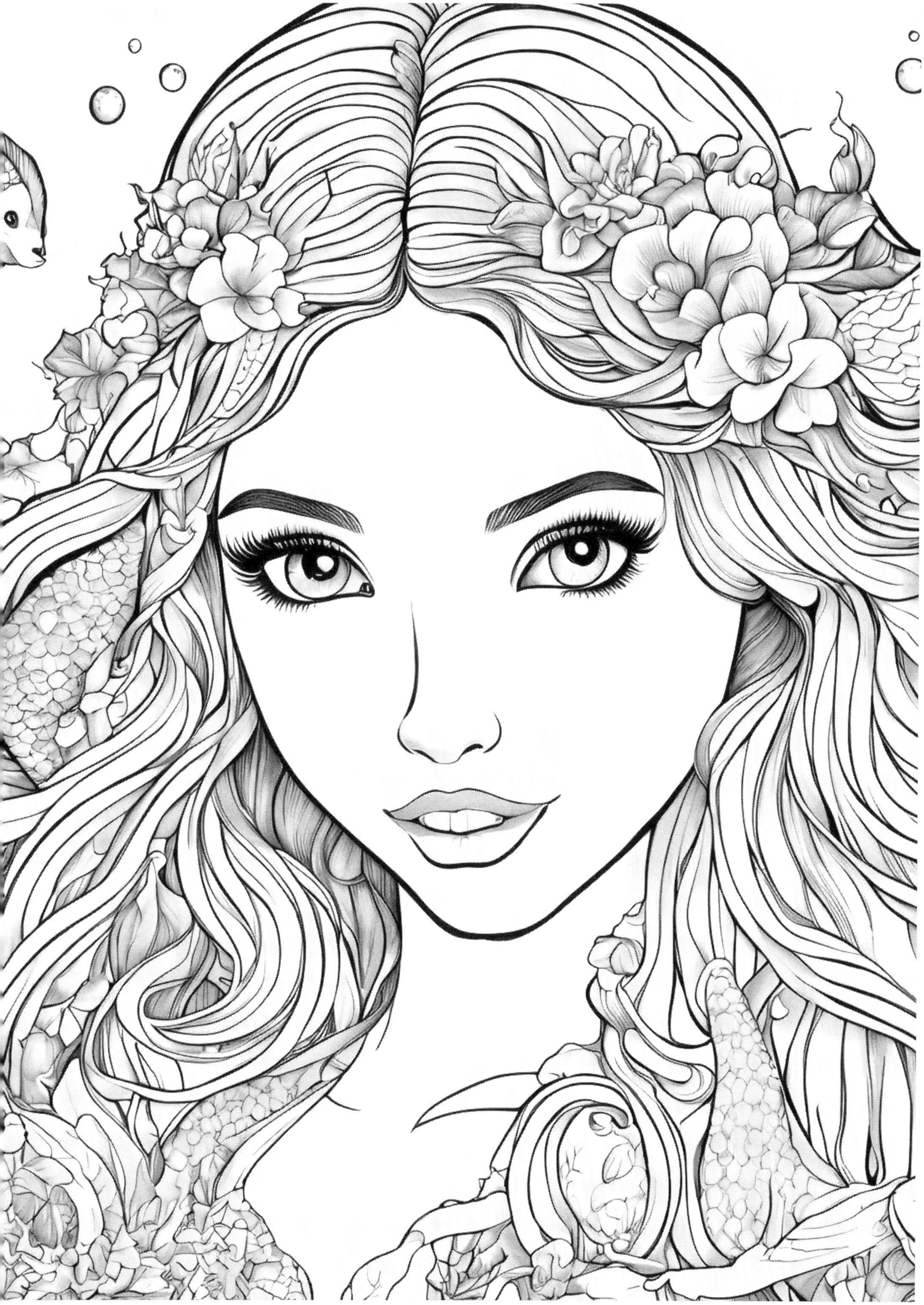

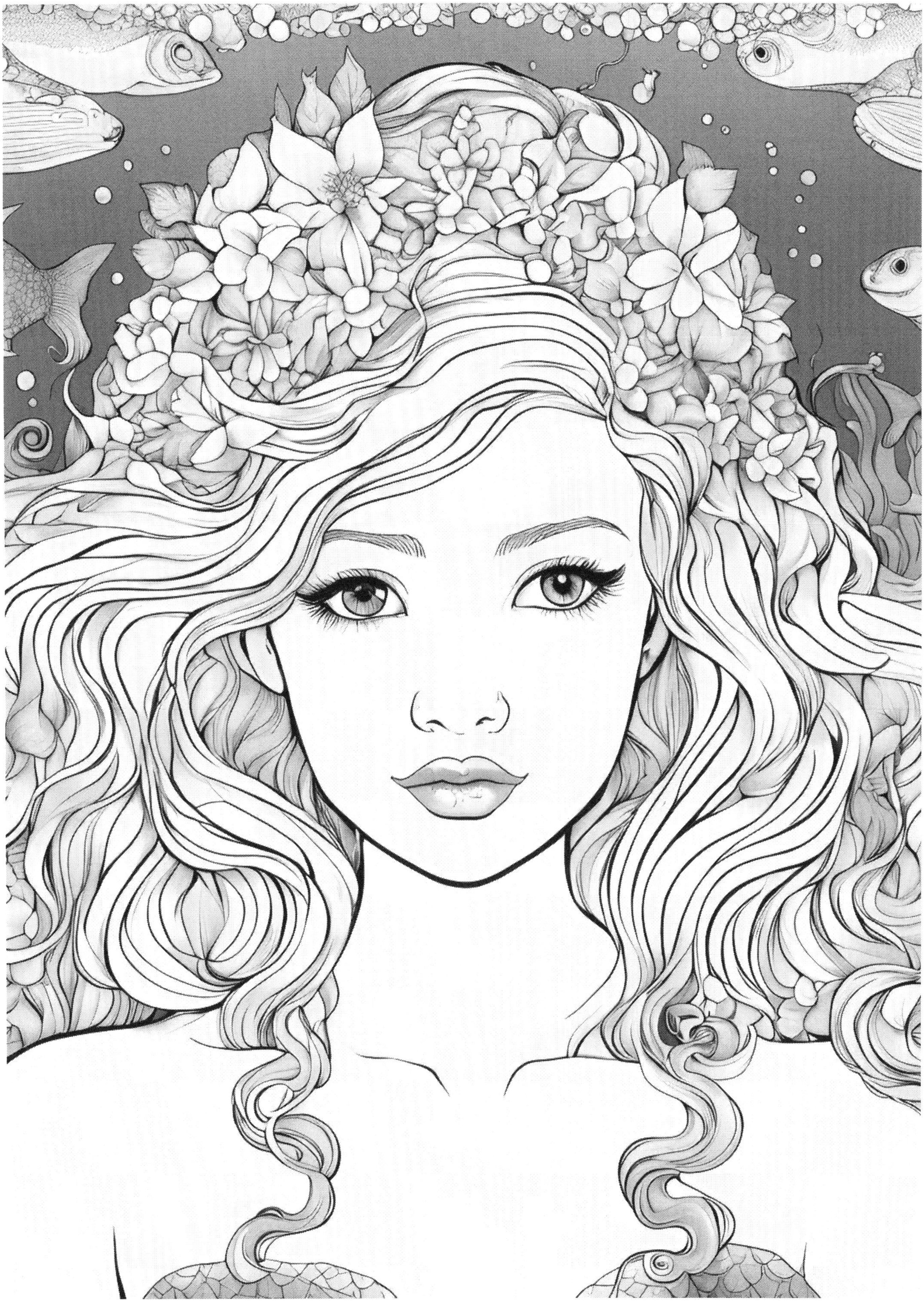

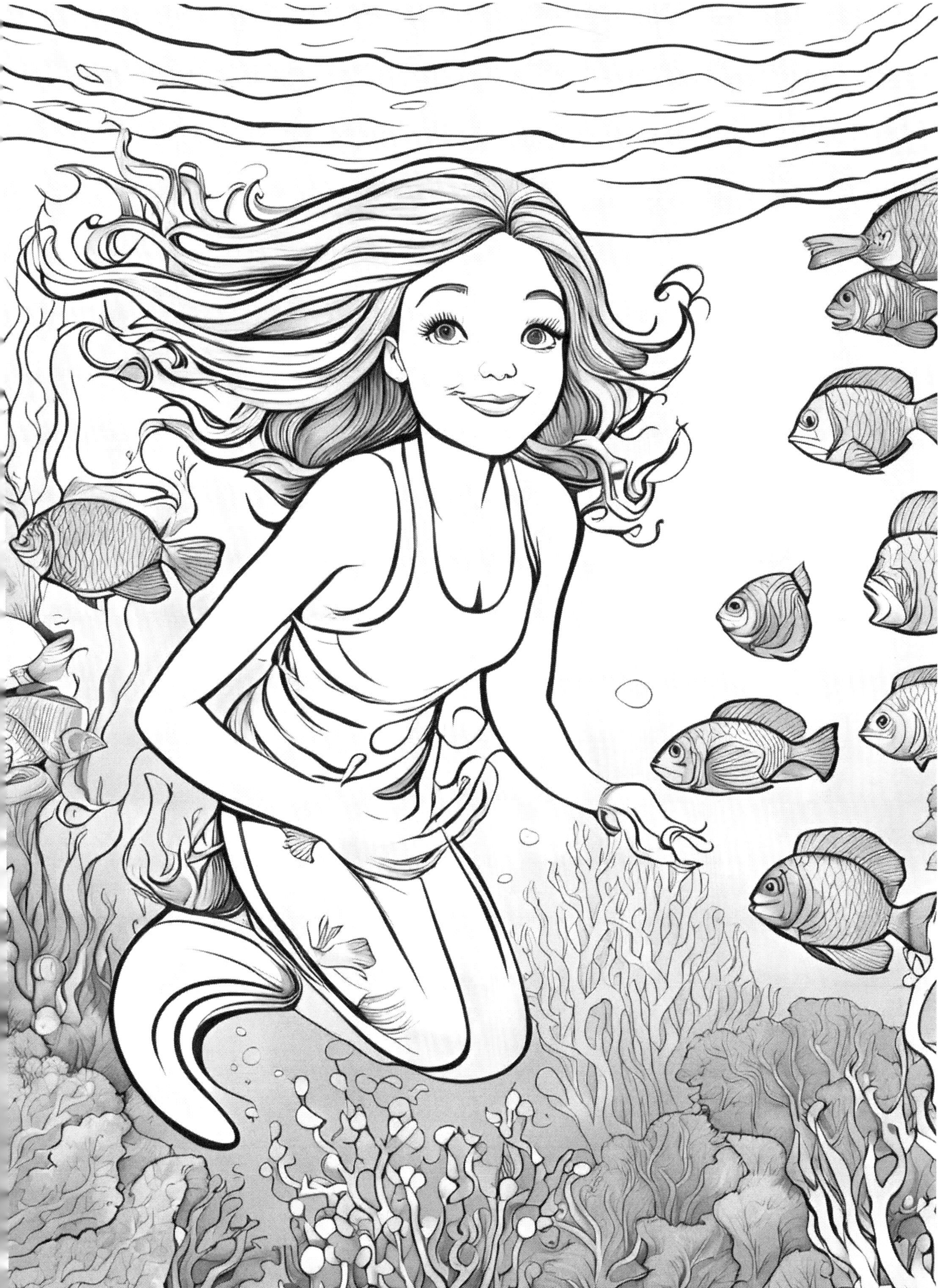

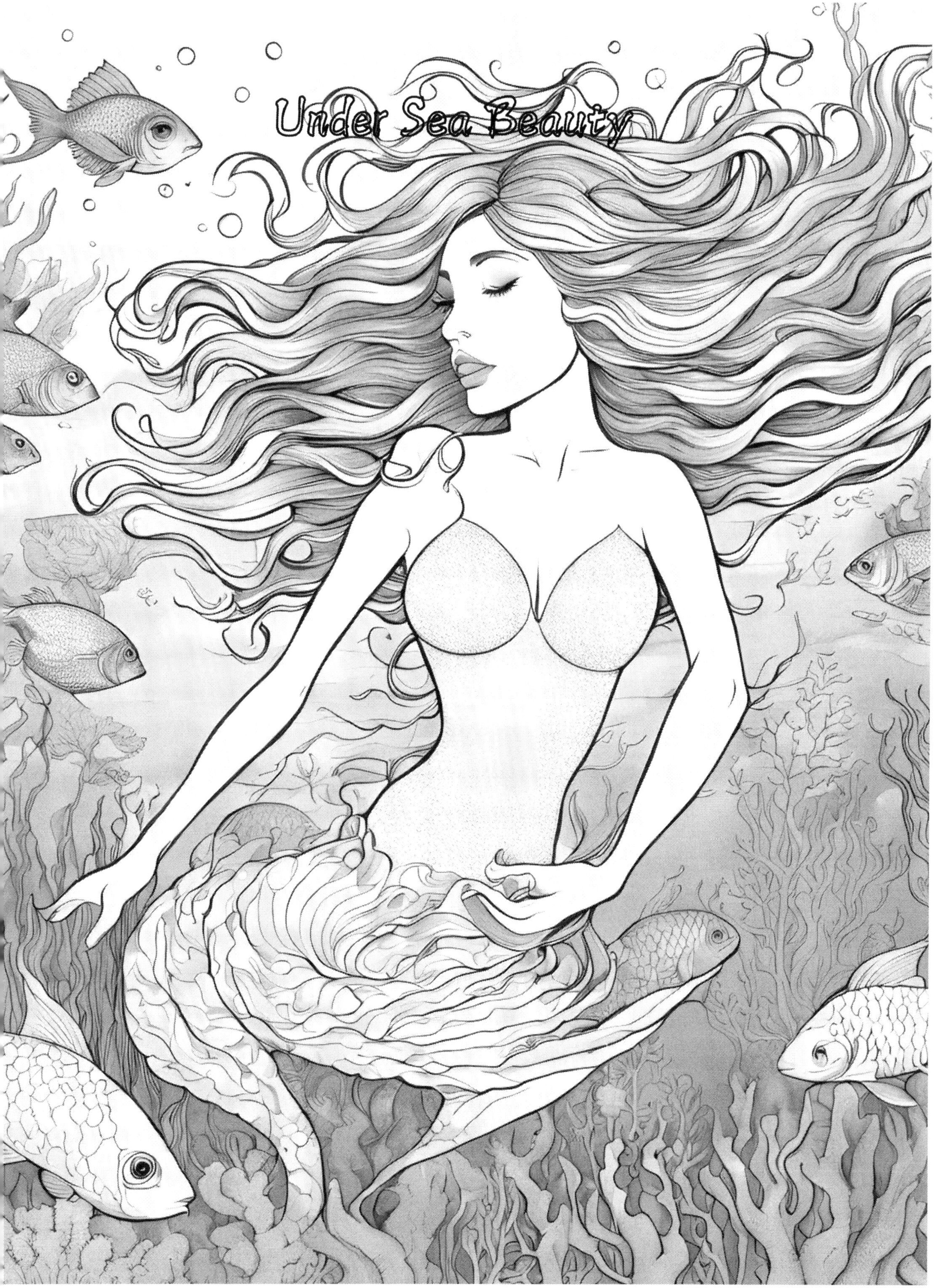
Under Sea Beauty

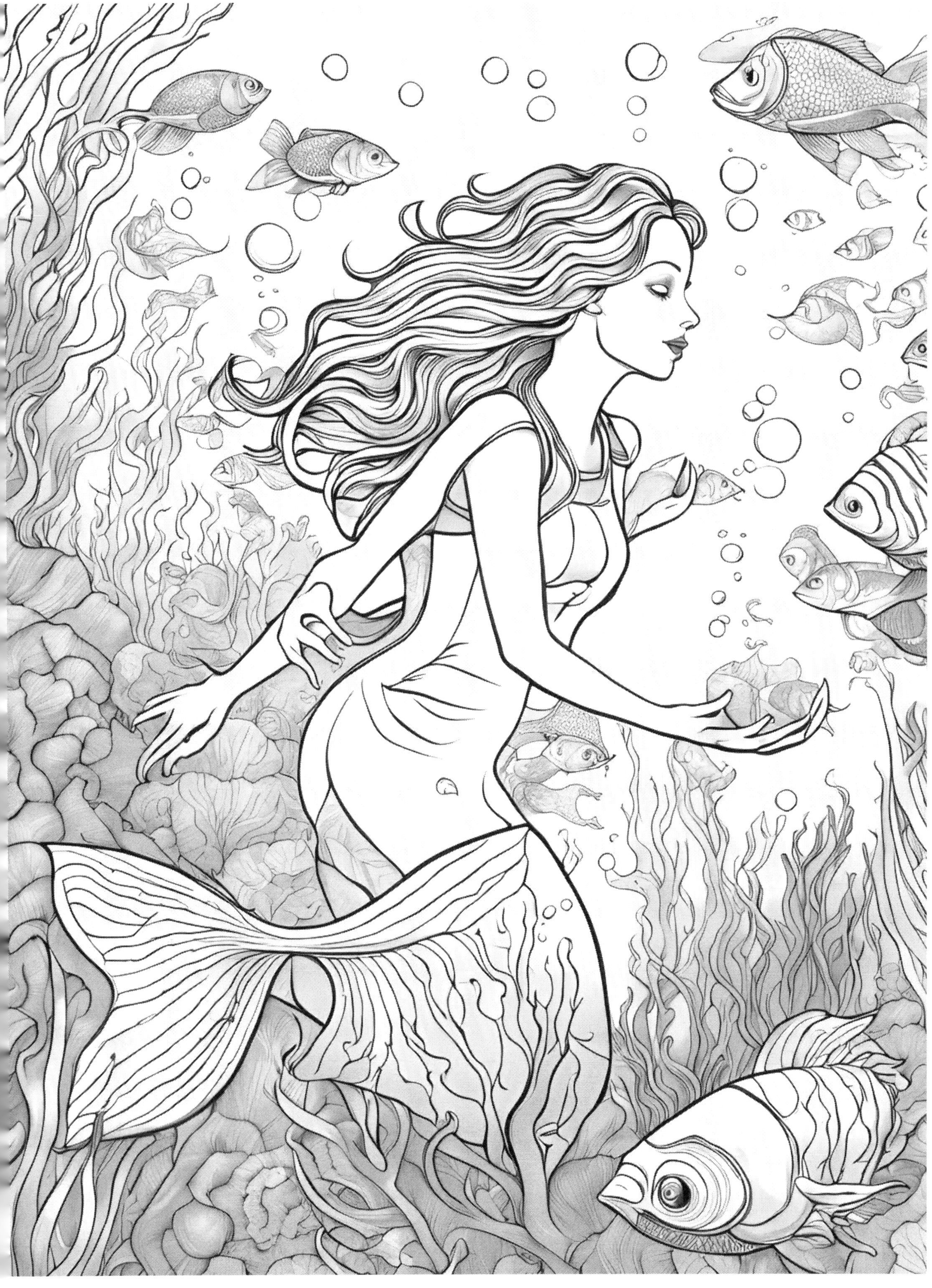

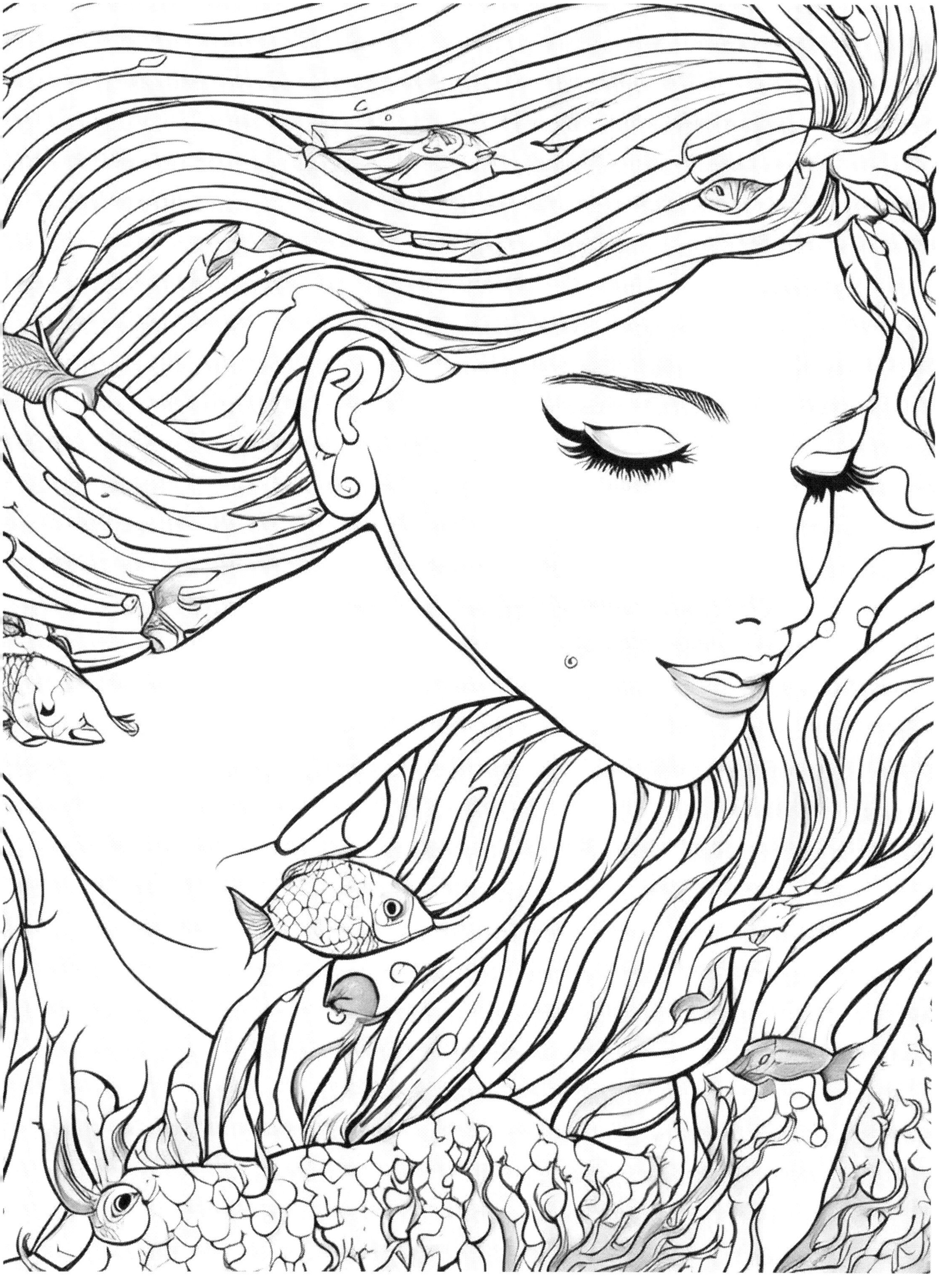

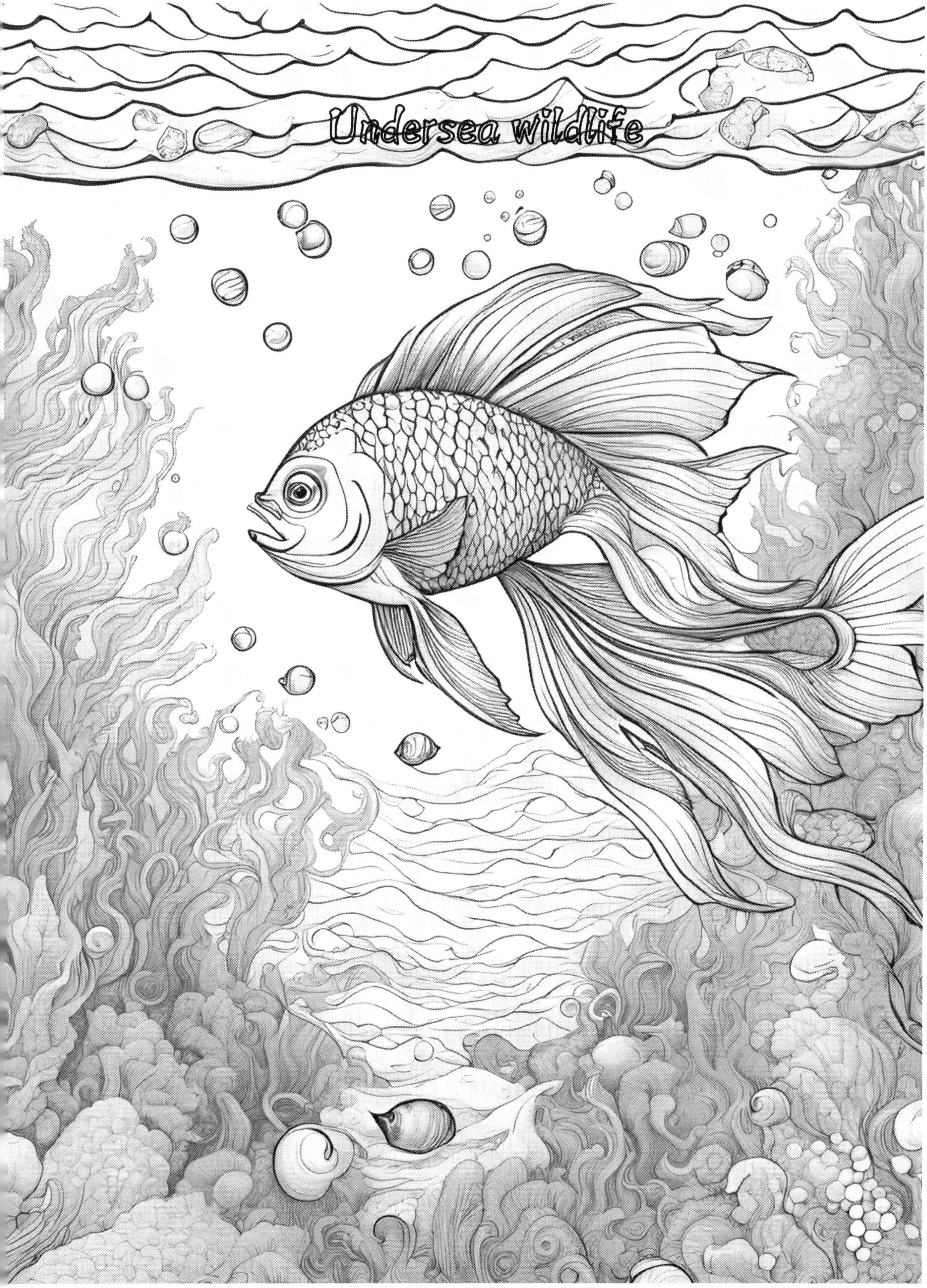
Undersea wildlife

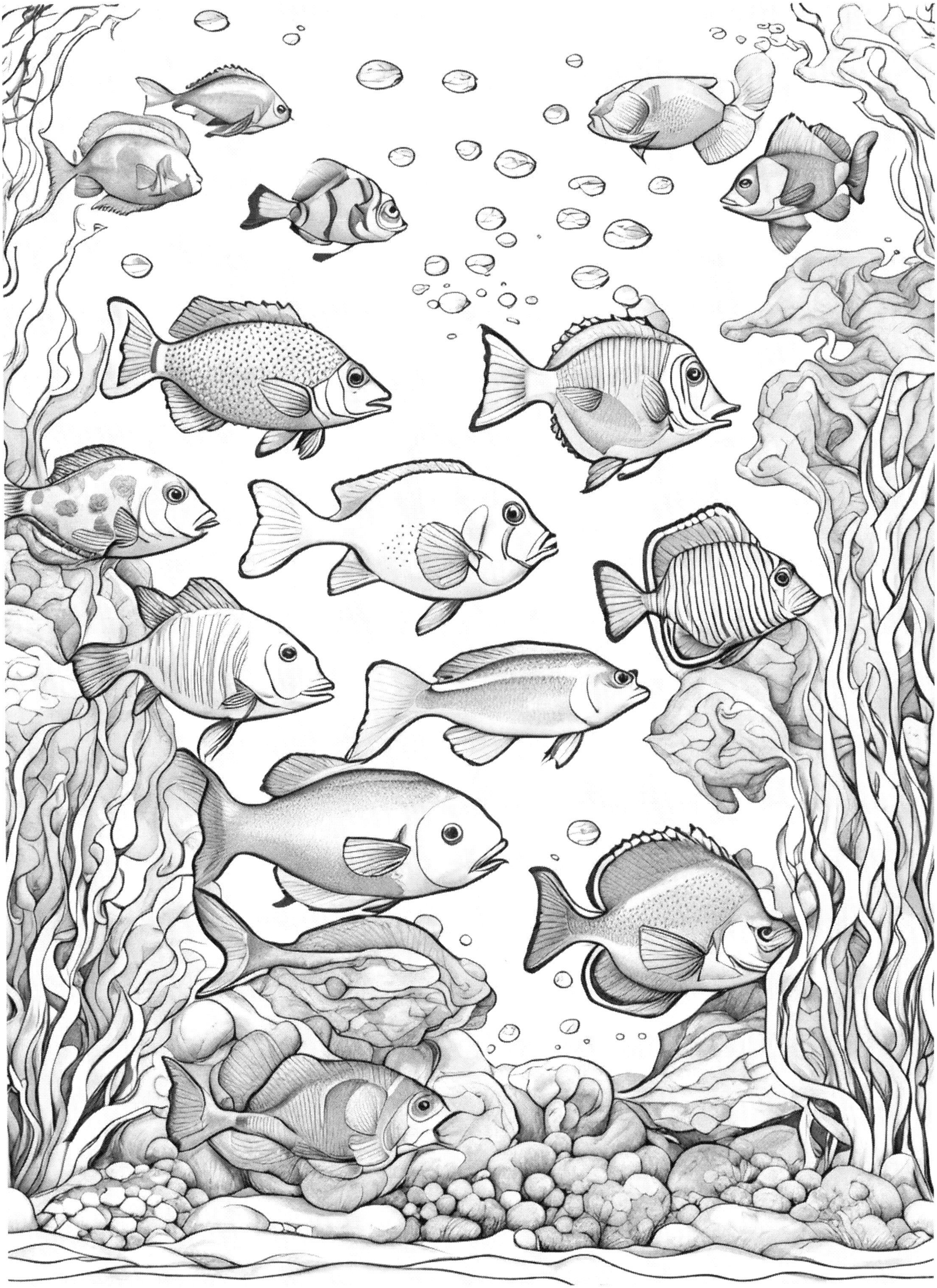

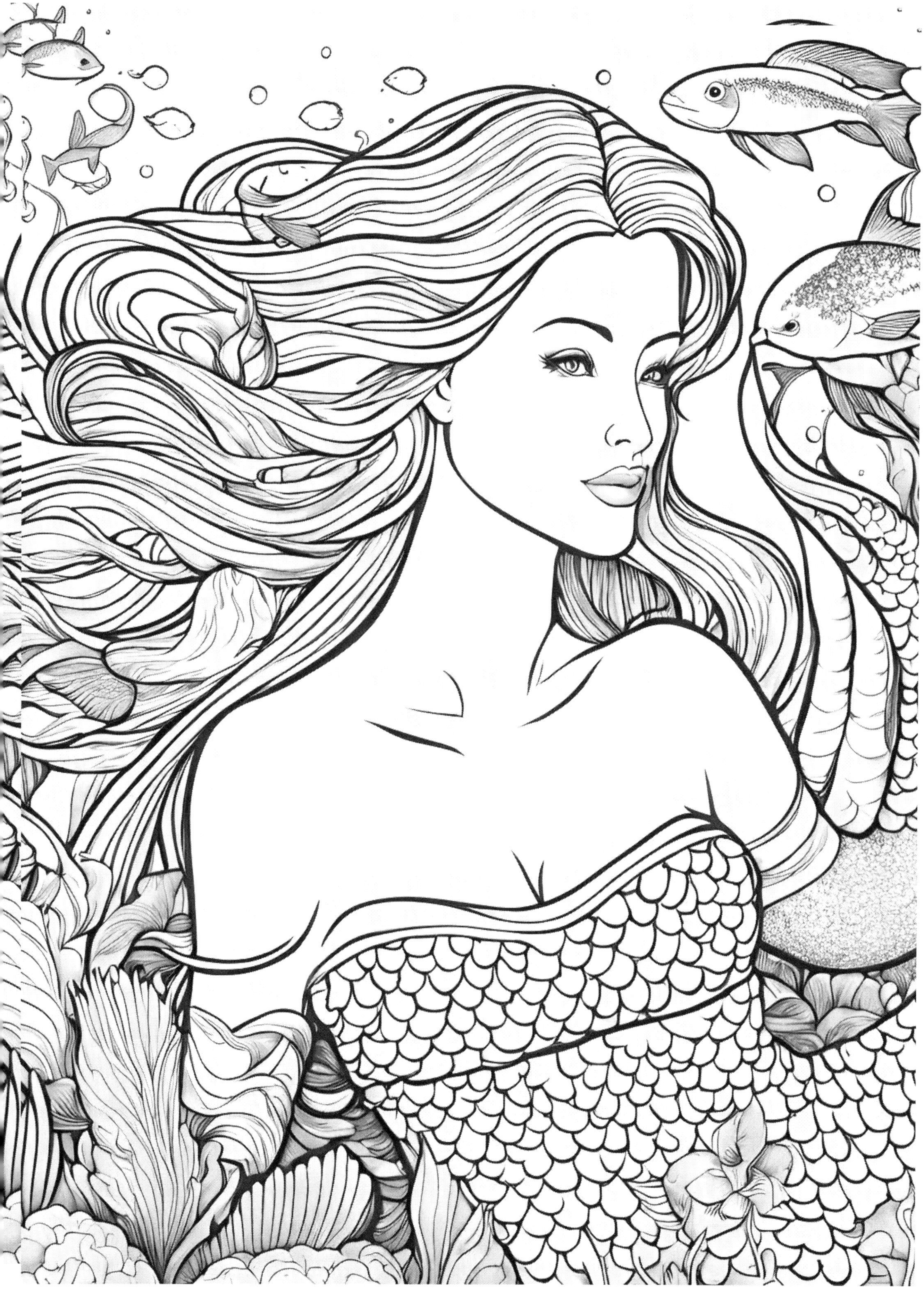

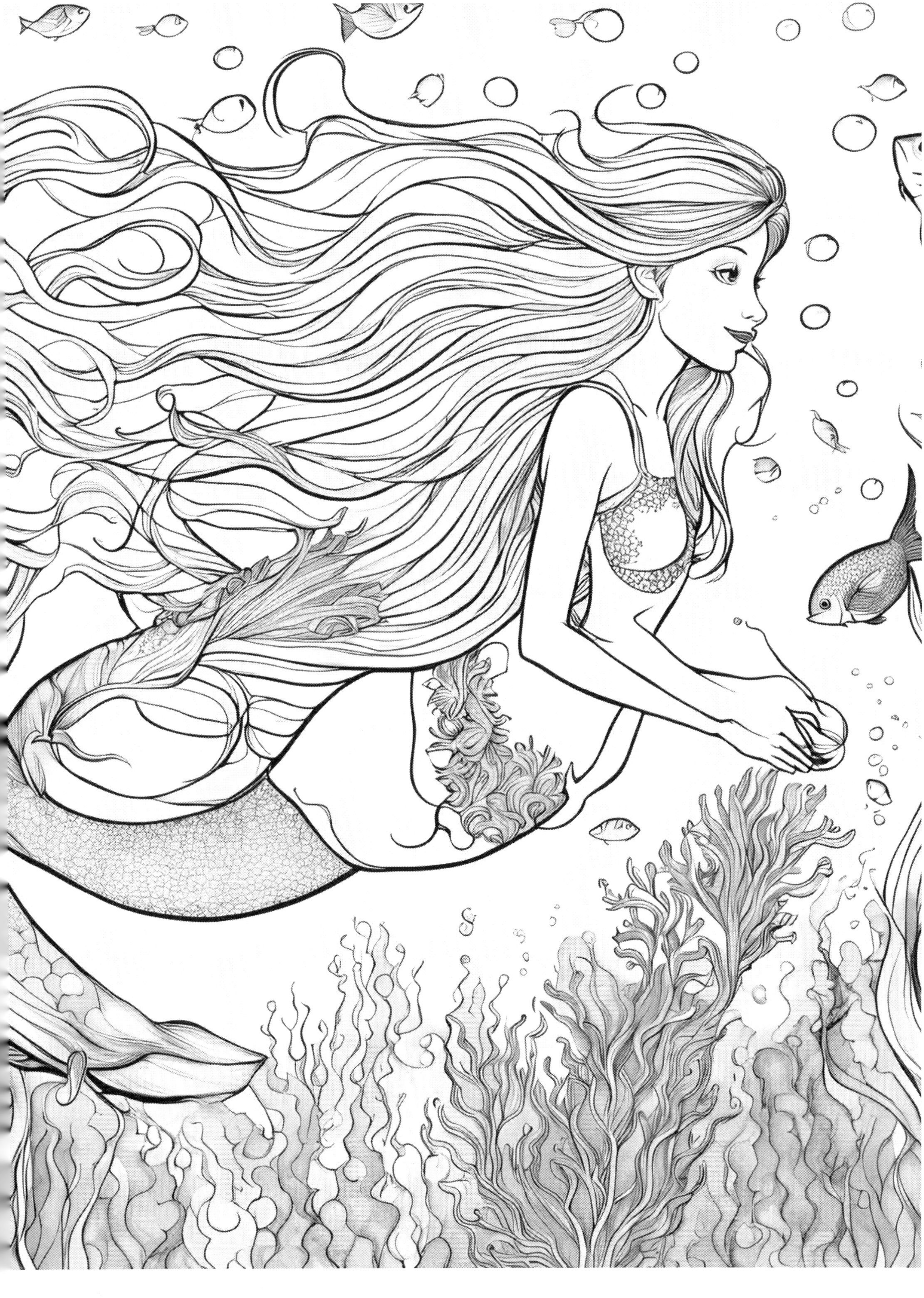

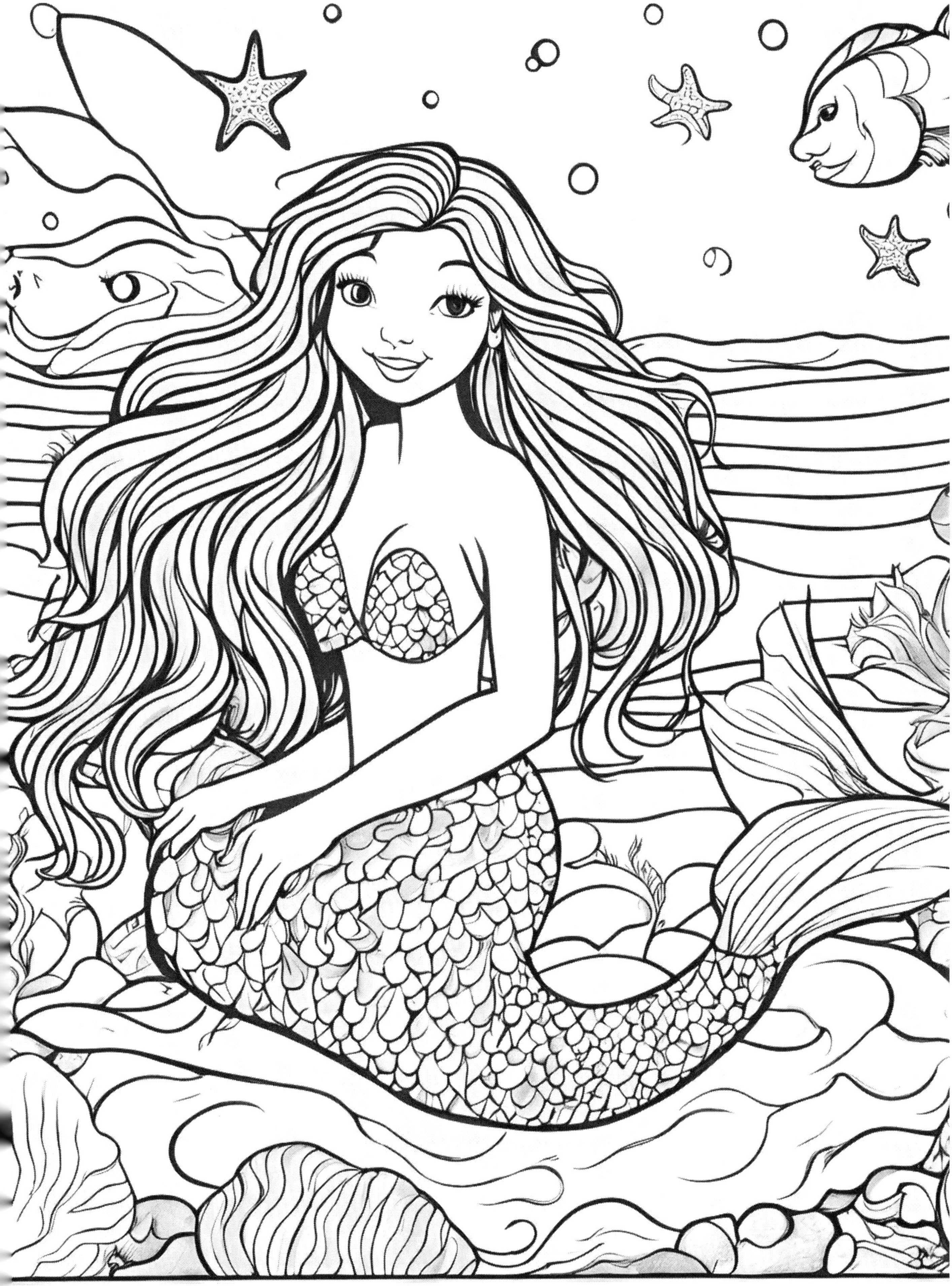

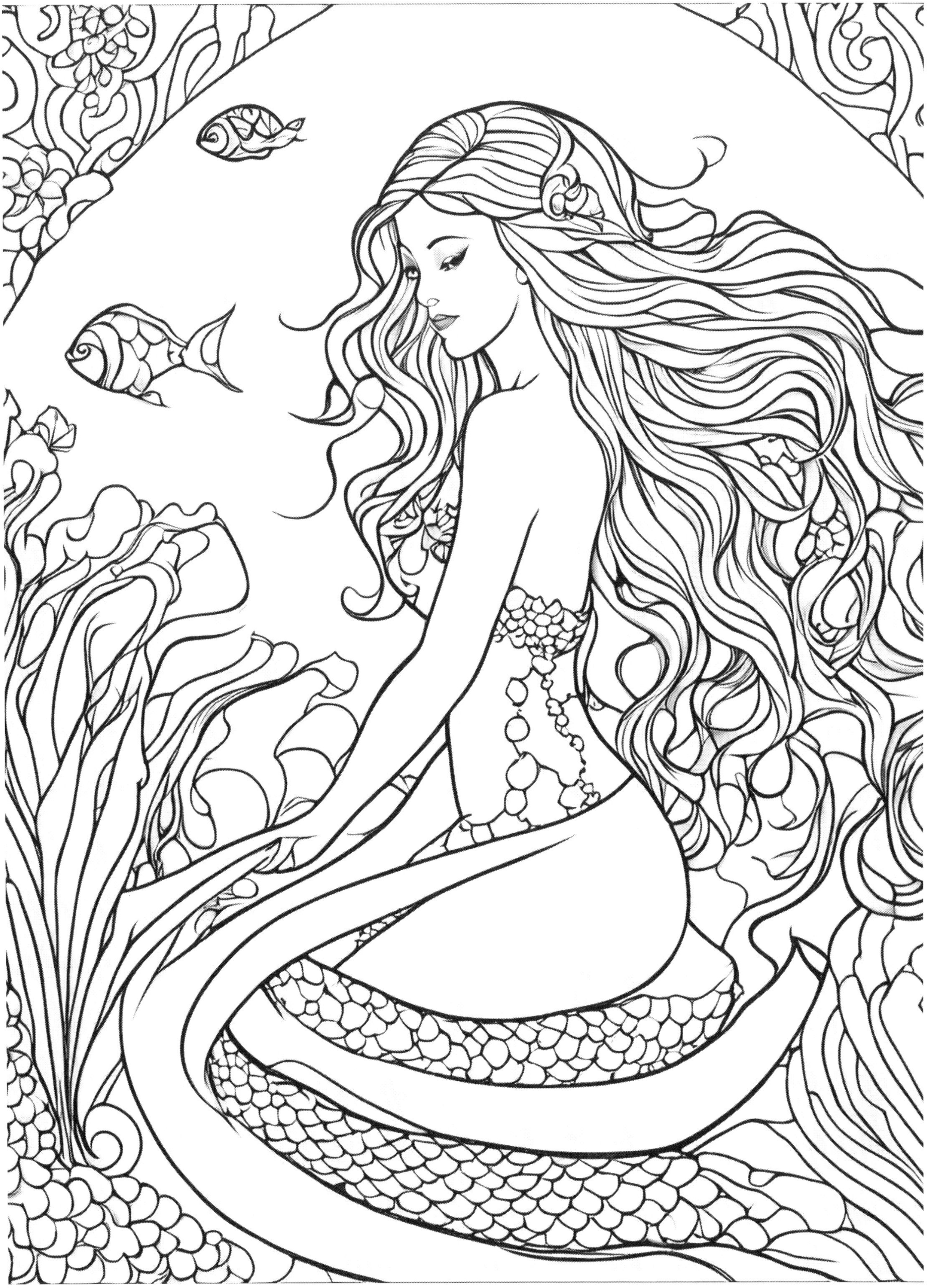

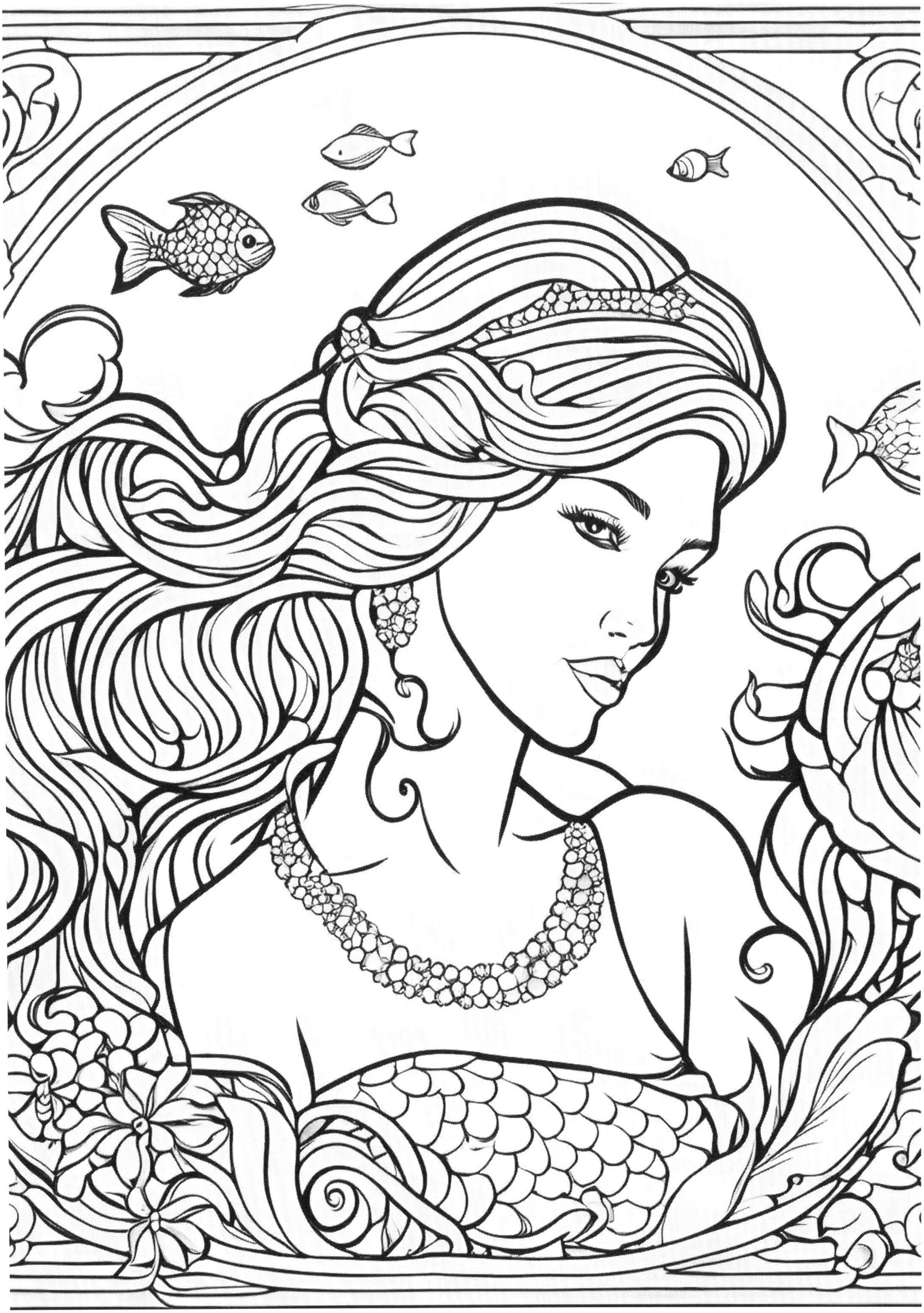

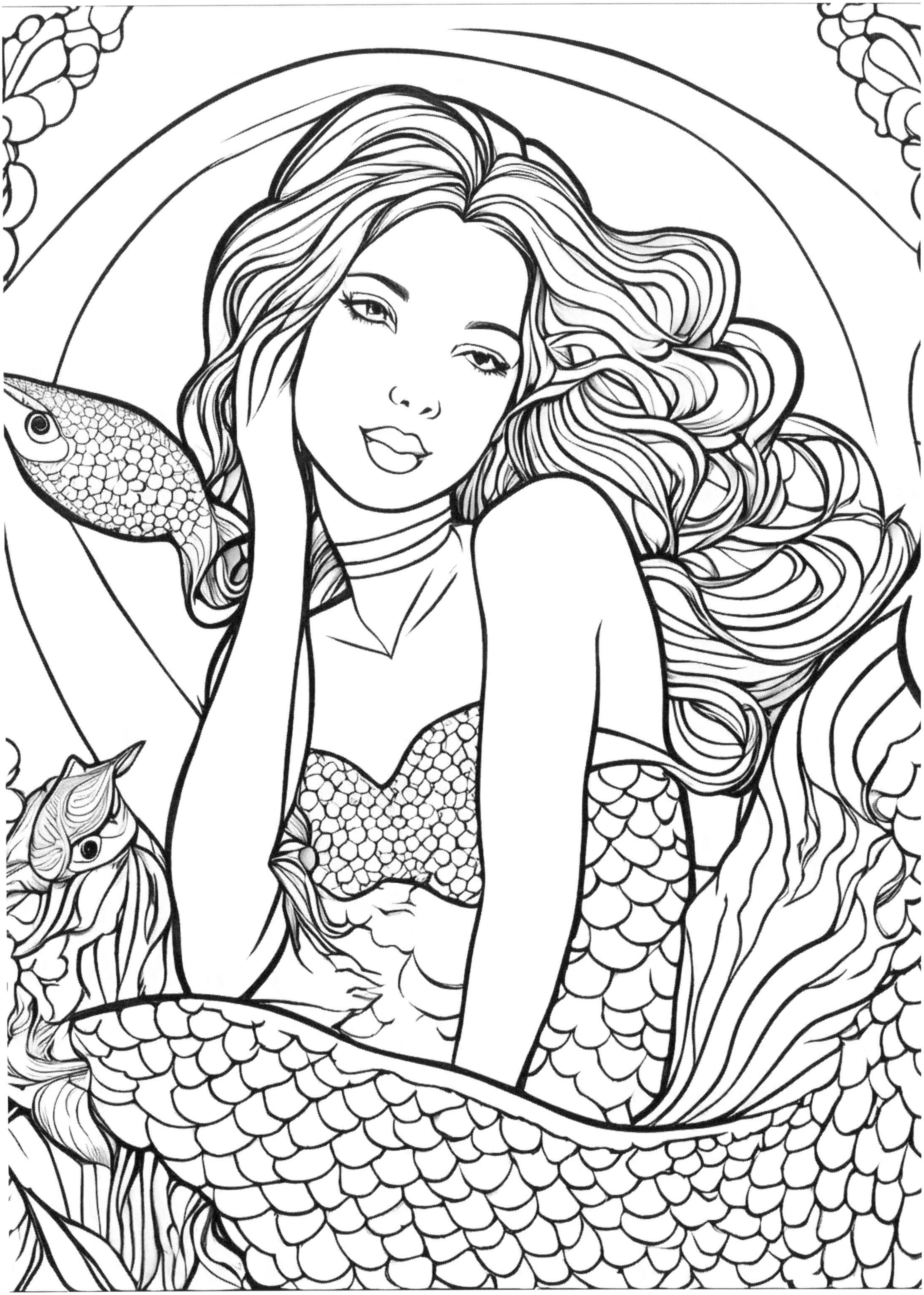

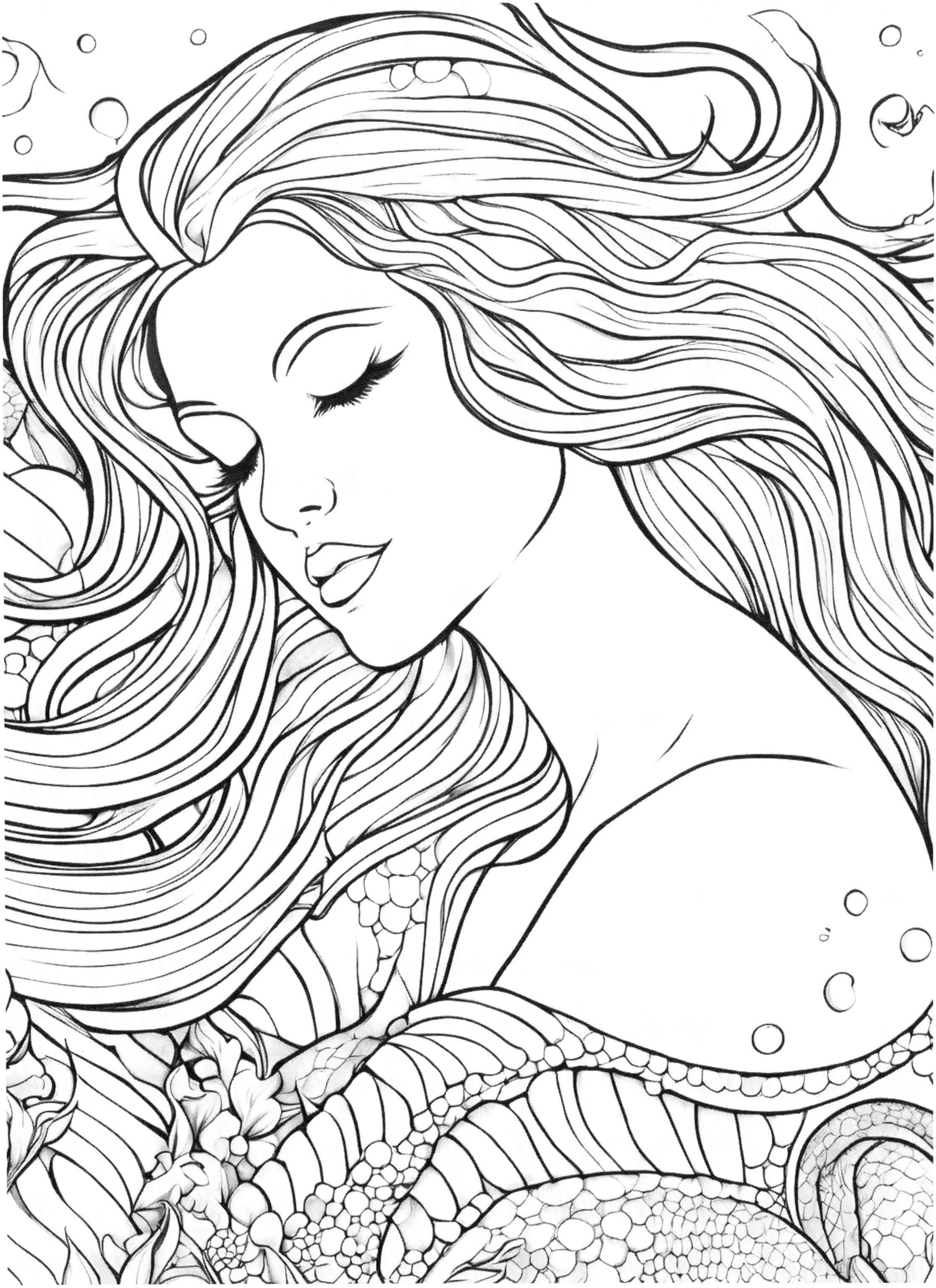

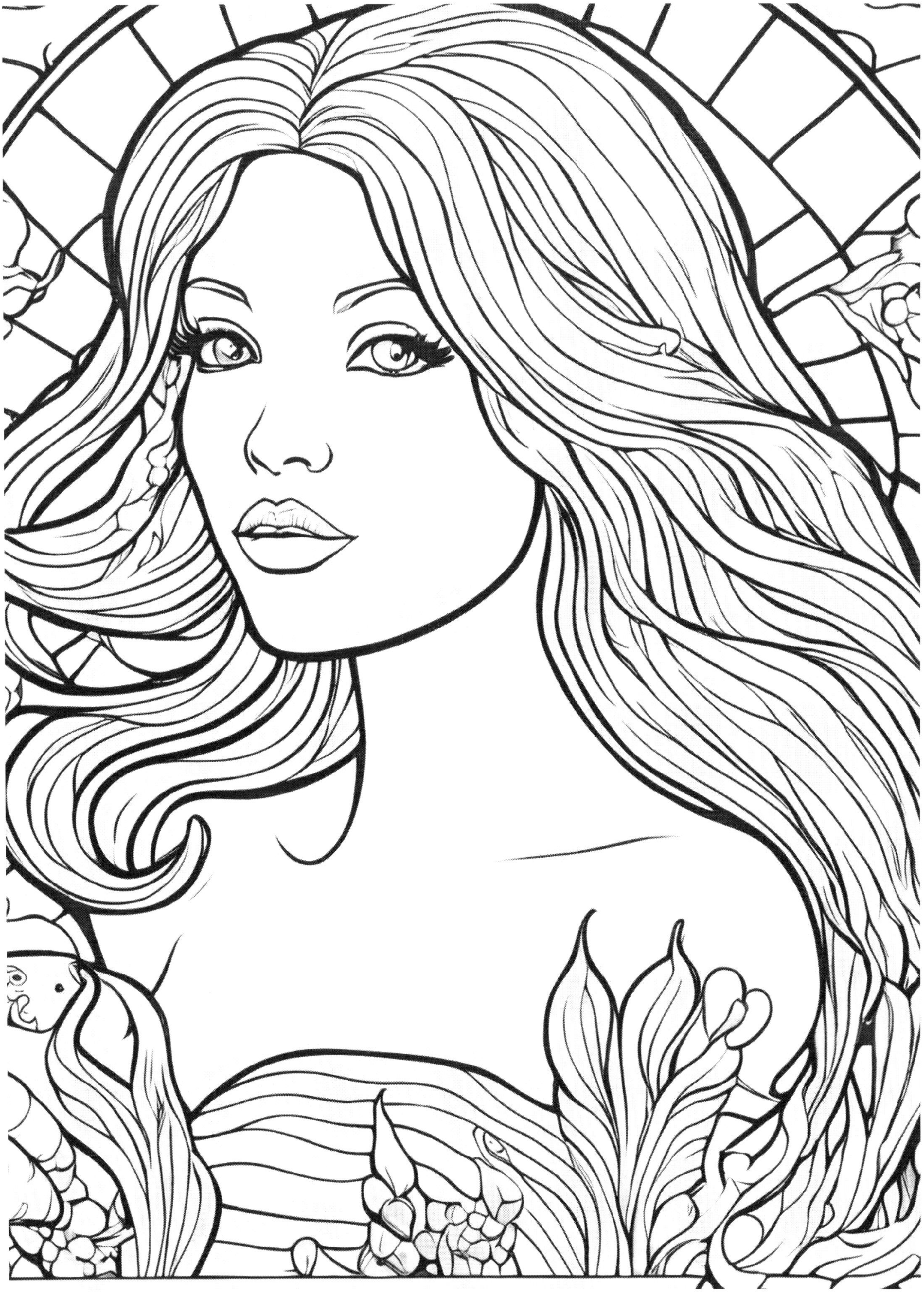

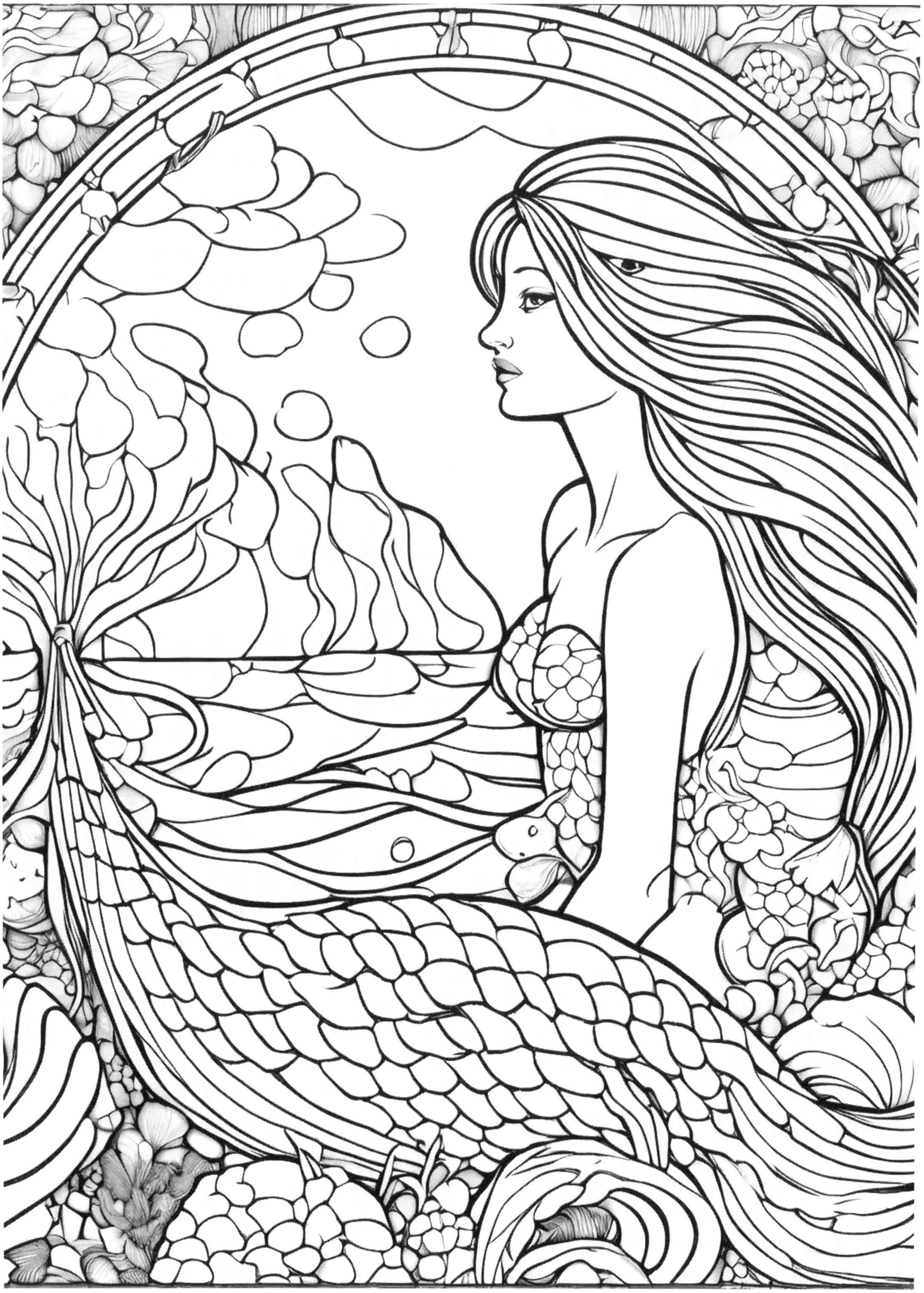

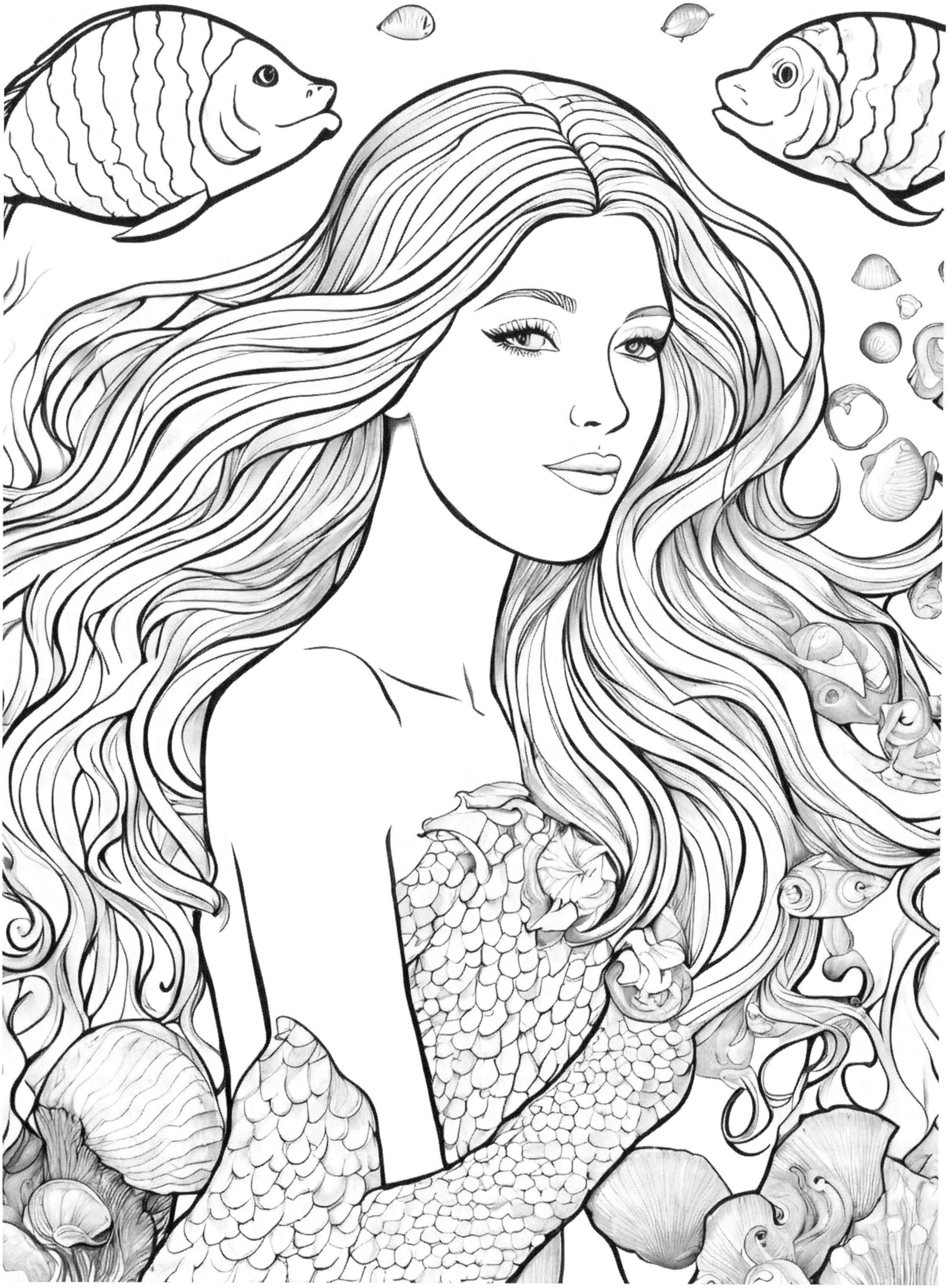

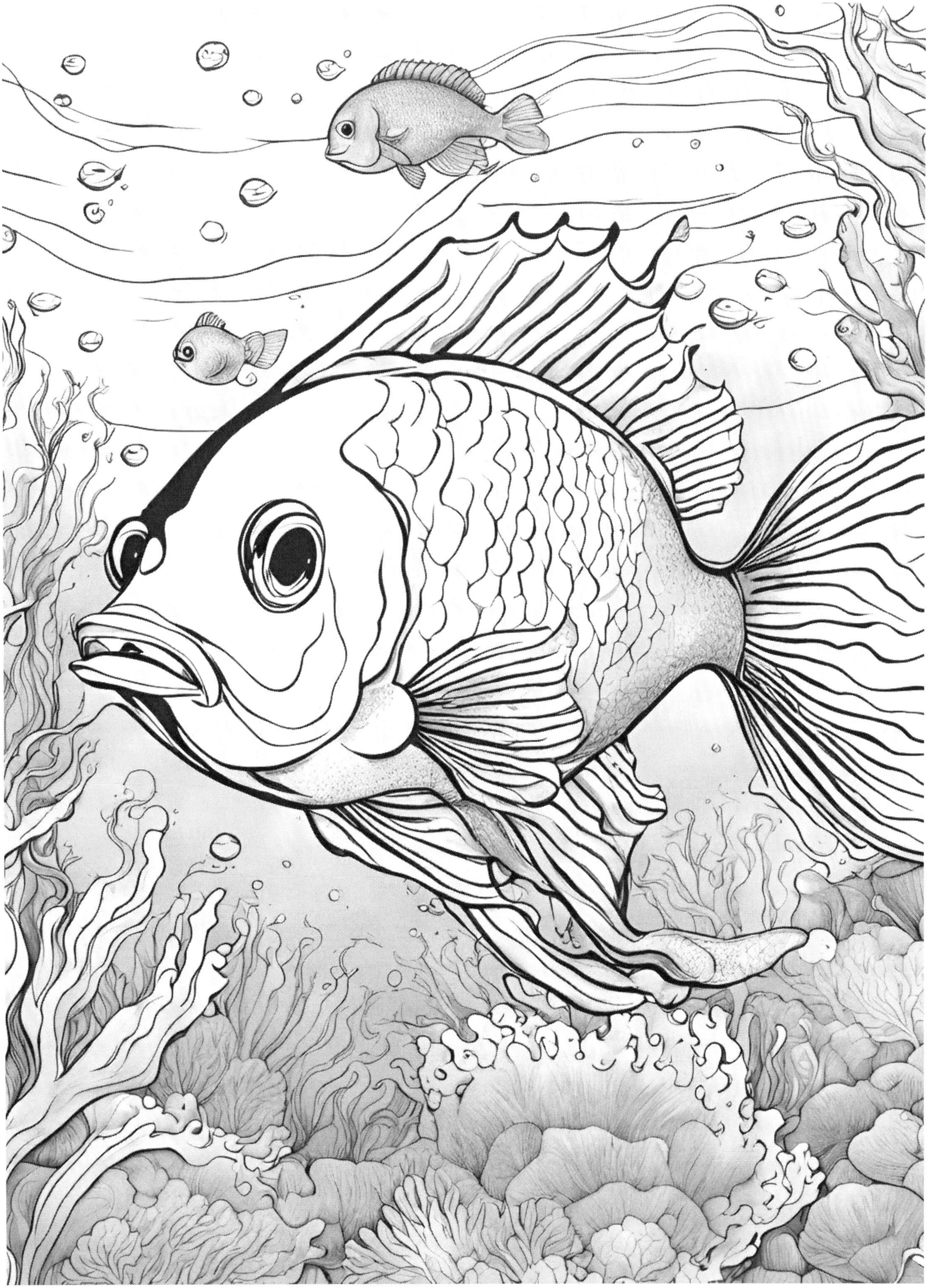

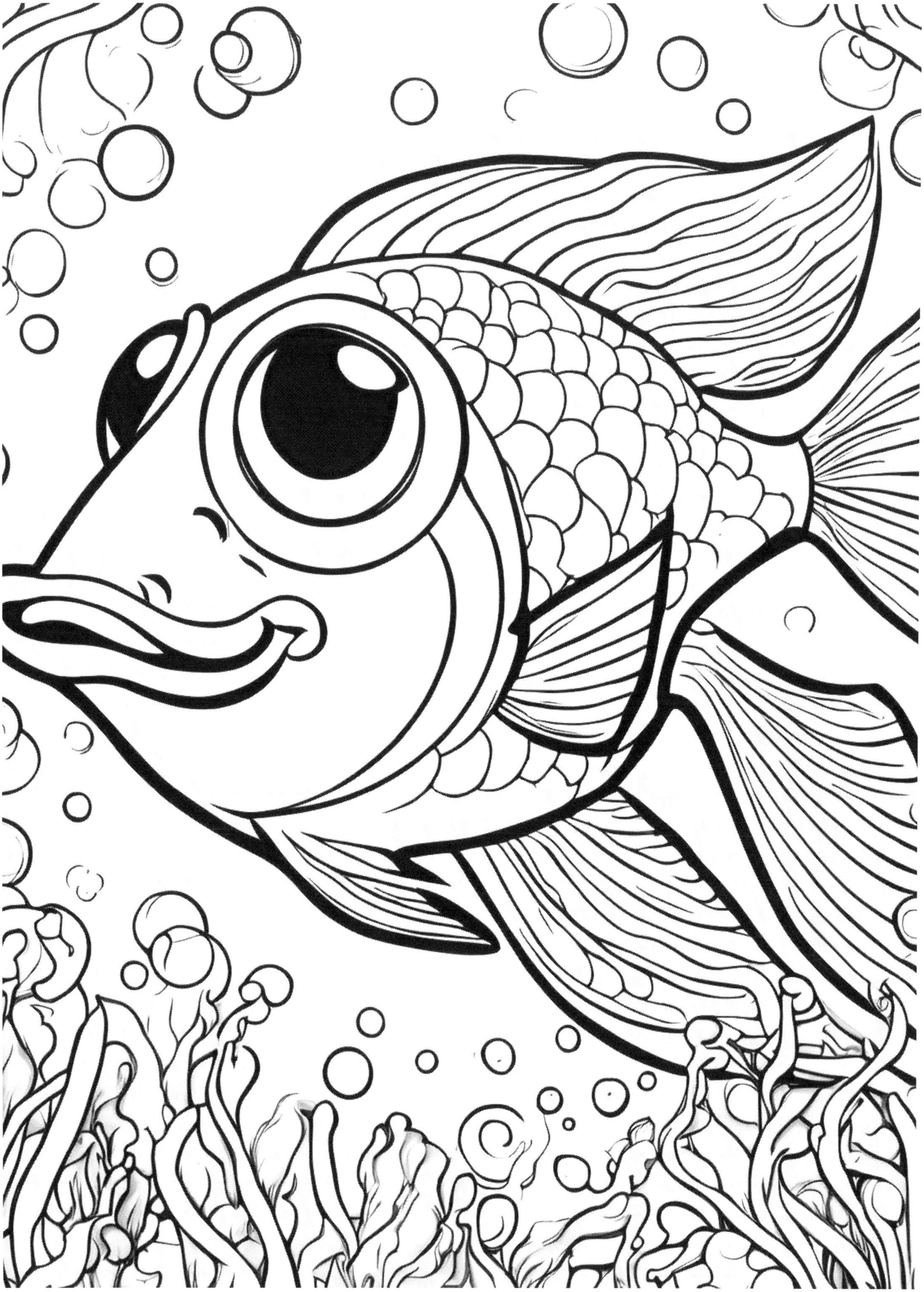

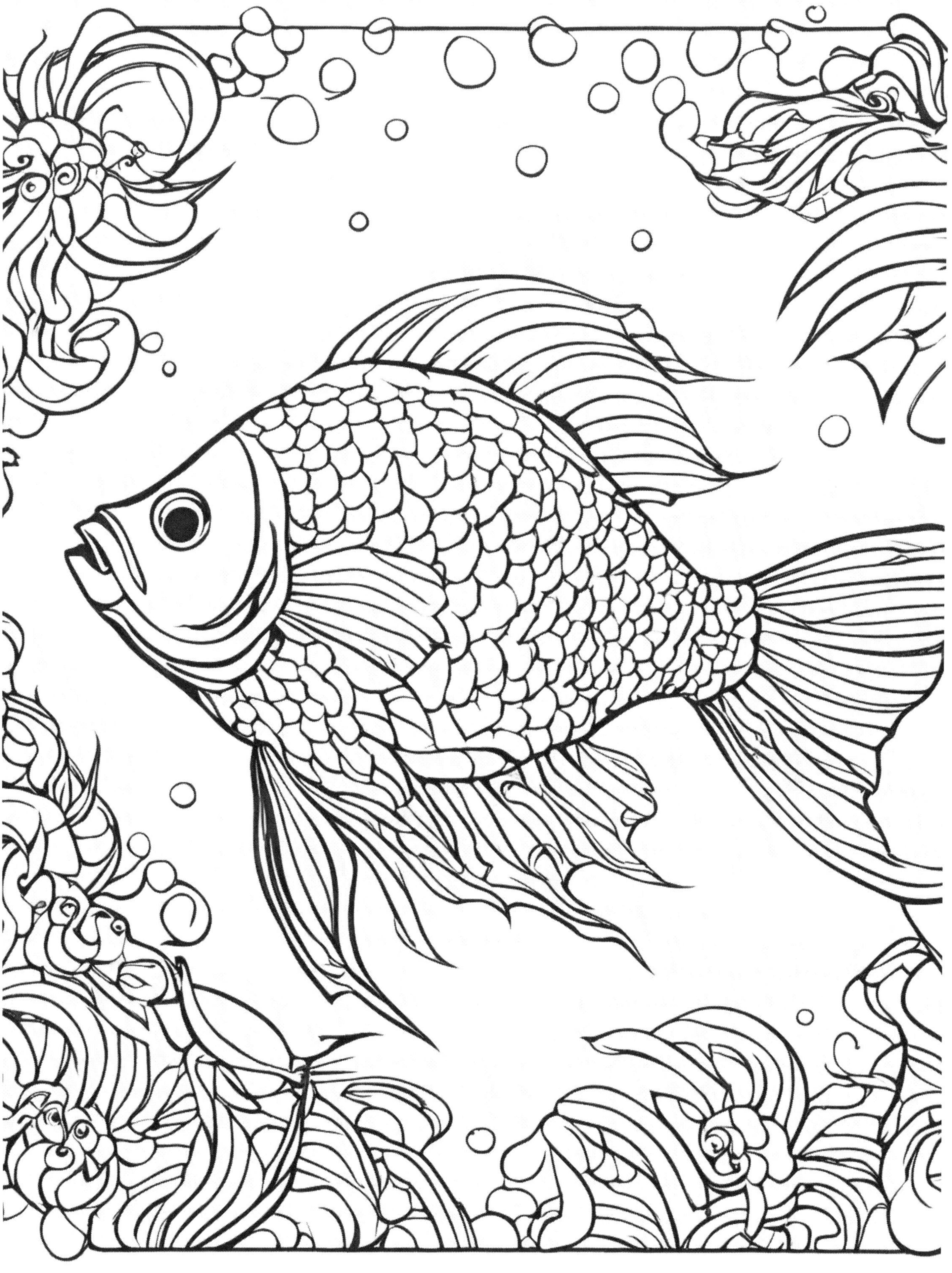

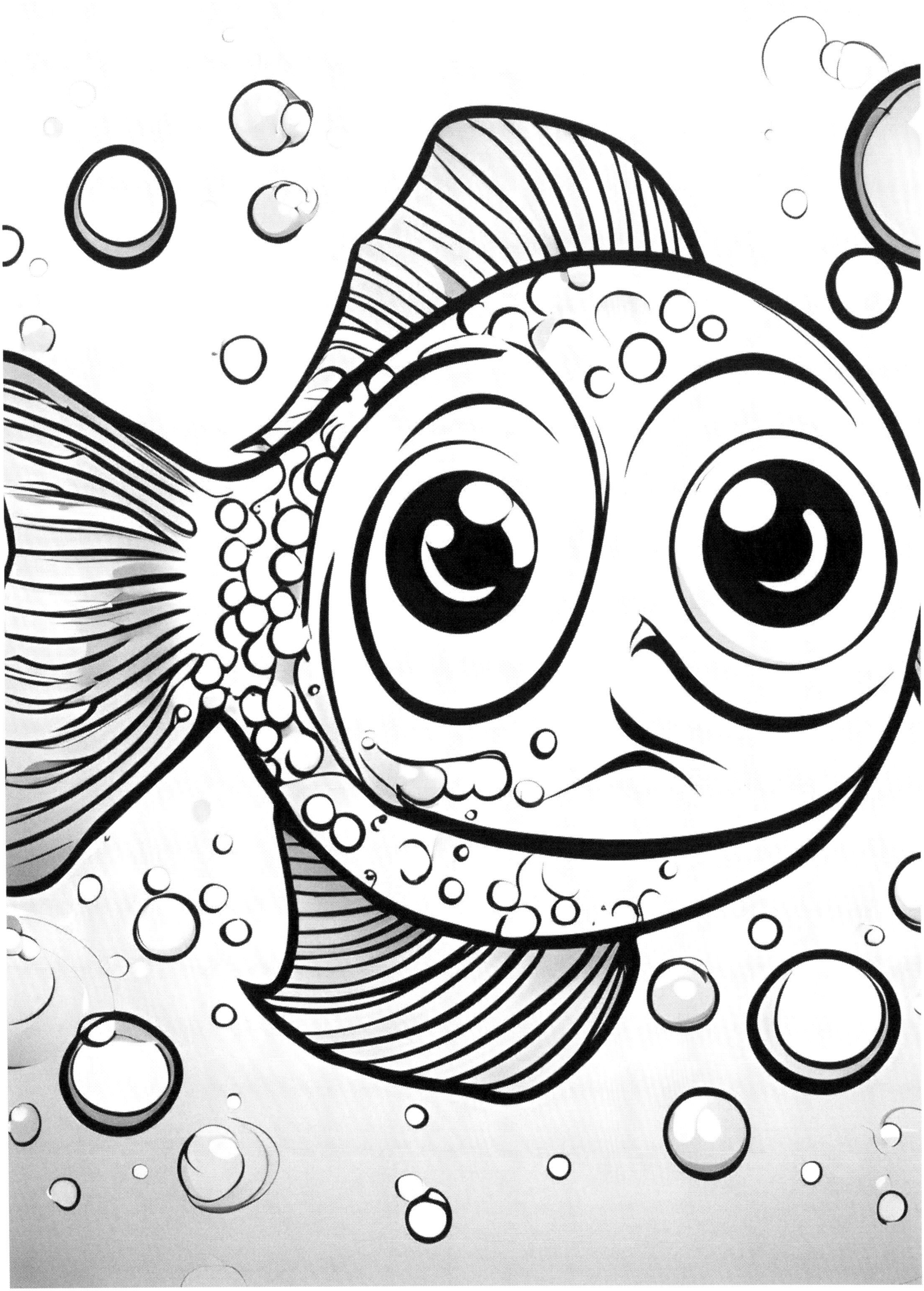

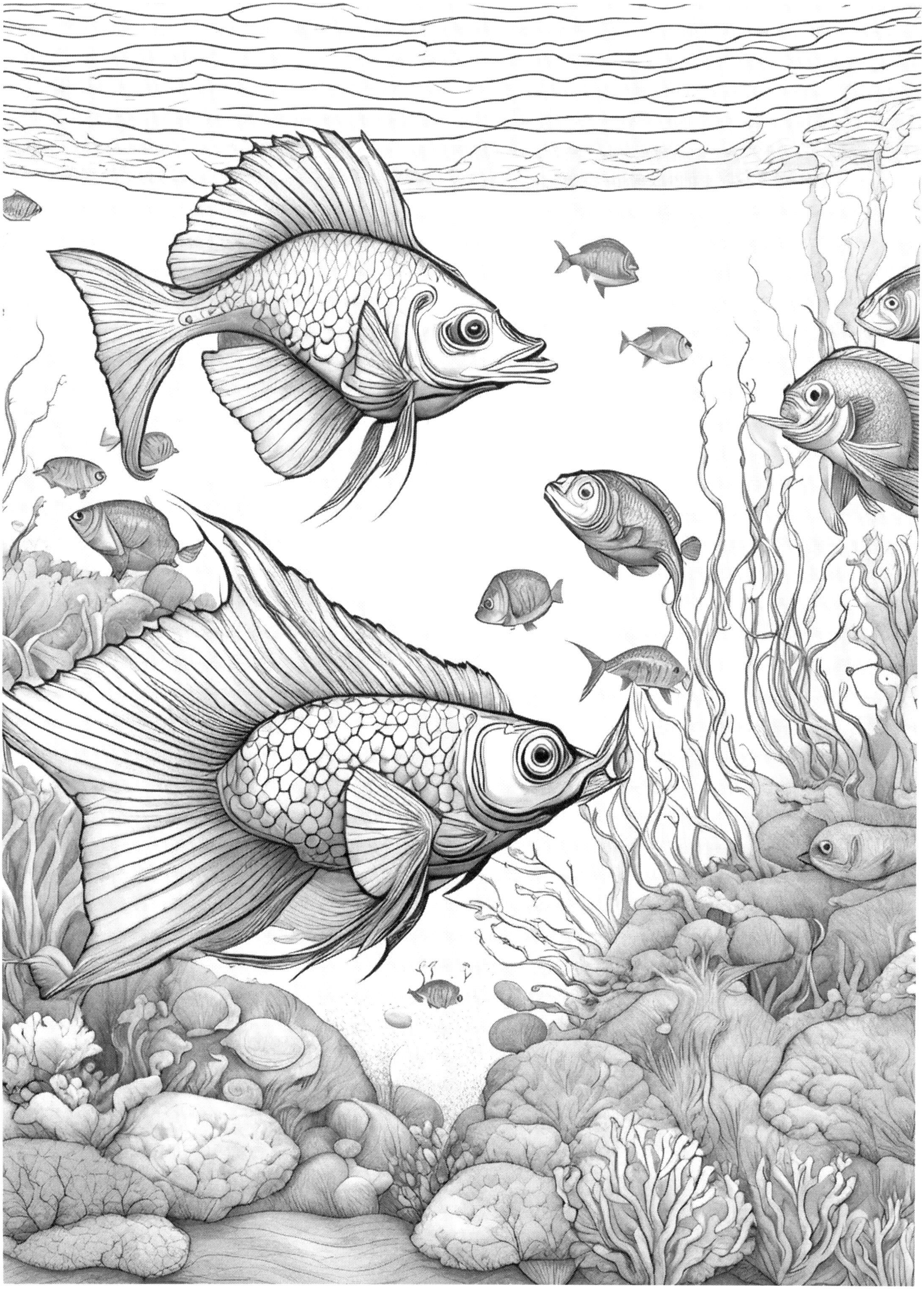

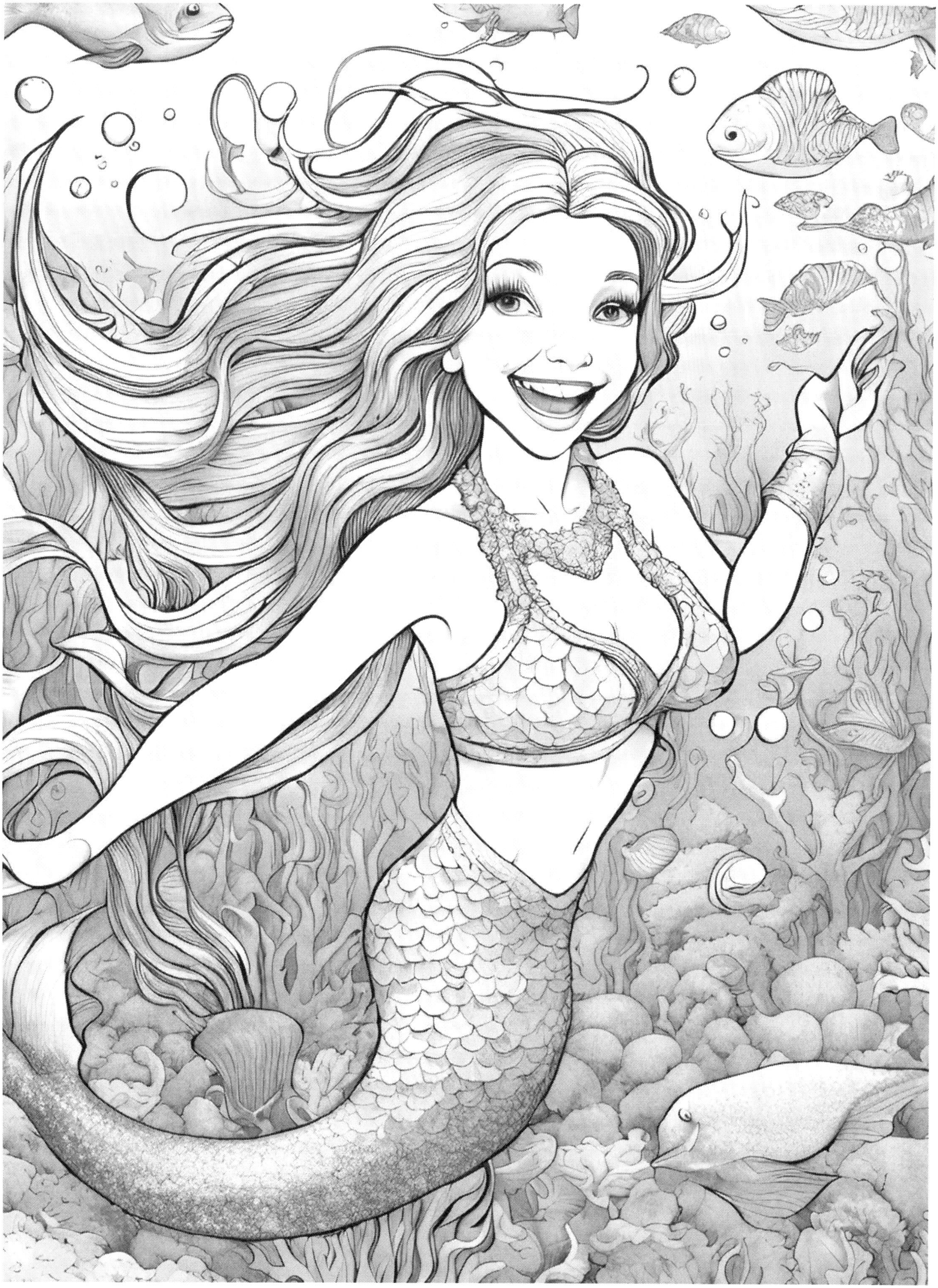

Made in the USA
Middletown, DE
15 January 2025

69535929R00031